Forgiveness

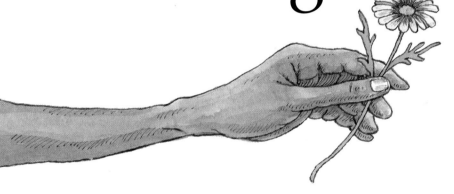

Forgiveness
The Story of Mahatma Gandhi

by

Mary Logue

Illustrated by

Robin Lawrie

The Child's World®

Library of Congress Cataloging-in-Publication Data
Logue, Mary.
Forgiveness: the story of Mahatma Gand [h] i / Mary Logue.
p. cm.
Summary: Emphasizes the value of forgiveness in this biog-
raphy of the Indian leader who led his country to freedom
from British rule through his policy of nonviolent resistance.

ISBN 1-56766-224-2

1. Gandhi, Mahatma, 1869-1948--Juvenile literature.
2. Statesmen--India-- Biography--Juvenile literature.
3. Nationalists--India--Biography--Juvenile literature.
[1. Gandhi, Mahatma. 1869-1948. 2. Statesmen.] I. Title.
DS481, G3L64 1996
954, 03'5'092
[B]--DC20
95-43783
CIP
AC r96

Contents

The First Lesson

Mohandas Gandhi was born in 1869 in a small town just north of Bombay, India. He was called Mohan. He was the youngest of six children. His family shared their house with his uncles, aunts, and cousins. Mohan's father was the town's *diwan*—the man who settles problems between people, like a judge.

Mohan learned about the Hindu religion from his mother. She took him to the Hindu temple. He watched her as she took care of the poor and the sick. His mother *fasted* for her religion. When she fasted, she would not eat for a day or so. Gandhi would use this method later in his life to make a political point.

Mohan was shy at school, but at home he was a rascal. He teased his sisters and got into all sorts of trouble.

When Mohan was only 13, he was married to a young girl named Kasturbai. Childhood marriages were not unusual in India. The two continued to live apart, in their parents' homes, until Kasturbai was done with school. Mohan tried to tell Kasturbai how to live her life, but she resisted him. He learned how effective this quiet resisting was and used it later against the British.

When he was 15, Mohan tried smoking and stole money from the servants. Then he stole a piece of his brother's jewelry. But Mohan felt bad about doing such things. He wrote a note to his father, telling him all that he had done. He asked his father to punish him. But his father did the opposite. To Gandhi's surprise, his father began to cry. Instead of punishing Mohan, his father forgave him.

It was a lesson Mohan would never forget.

What Is *Forgiveness?*

Suppose a friend stole an apple from you and ate it. If you said, "That's okay," you would be *forgiving* him. Forgiving someone means you will not be mad at them for what they have done. You are showing them that you care about them. You are giving them another chance.

Off to England

The Hindus believed in a *caste system*. They believed that some people were better than others. They divided people into five groups: PRIESTS, WARRIORS, MERCHANTS, ARTISANS, and UNTOUCHABLES. The Untouchables were the poorest people. No one would even talk to them. Mohan's family belonged to the caste of Merchants, or storekeepers.

When he was 18, Mohan's family decided to send him to college in England. At this time, England ruled India. When the leader of the Merchant caste found out, he was angry. No one from their caste had ever left the country to go to school! But Mohan stood up to him and said he would go anyway. The leader had Mohan thrown out of the Merchant caste. He said that no one was ever to speak to Mohan again.

Mohan never held this against the man. And he never tried to be part of the caste again.

Mohan lived in England for three years and became a lawyer. He had promised his mother he would not eat meat or drink alcohol. He kept both of his promises.

He had trouble being a vegetarian in England, where everyone ate meat. For the first few months, he lived on bread, oatmeal, and cocoa. Finally, he found a vegetarian restaurant and was able to eat a real meal. Gandhi would remain a vegetarian for the rest of his life. He ate only fruit, vegetables, and bread.

Another habit Gandhi picked up in England was walking. He walked everywhere he went in London. This habit saved him money and kept him in good shape. Years later, he would be able to walk younger men off their feet!

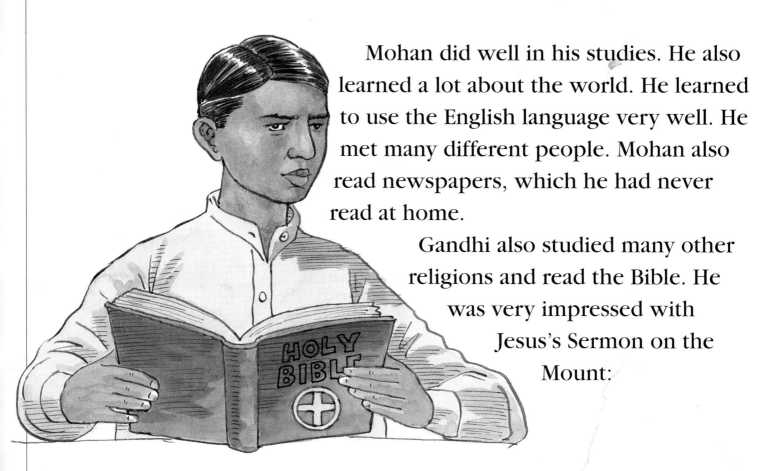

Mohan did well in his studies. He also learned a lot about the world. He learned to use the English language very well. He met many different people. Mohan also read newspapers, which he had never read at home.

Gandhi also studied many other religions and read the Bible. He was very impressed with Jesus's Sermon on the Mount:

"Whosoever shall smite thee on thy right cheek, turn to him the other also. And if any man take away thy coat, let him have thy cloak also."

Mohan Gandhi was continuing to learn the lesson of forgiveness.

A verse that Mohan Gandhi learned as a child:
But the truly noble know all men as one,
And return with gladness good for evil done.
This means that if someone does something bad to you, you do something nice to them.

A Lawyer in South Africa

In 1891, Gandhi returned from England. He was glad to be home, but bad news awaited him. His mother had died a few months before he left England. Gandhi was sad. His mother would never know that he had kept his promises to her and finished his law degree.

When Gandhi went to work as a lawyer in India, he was not very successful. He knew English law, but not Indian law.

In 1893, he was sent to South Africa to handle a case. It was not easy to be an Indian in this country. In parts of South Africa, Indians could not own land or run a business. It was even against the law for them to go for a walk after nine o'clock at night!

One day, Gandhi boarded a train with a first-class ticket. He was asked to leave the first-class section because he was not white. When he refused, a policeman threw him off the train. He had to sit overnight in a railway station. He had a lot of time to think. He decided to fight this discrimination against Indians.

Gandhi lived in South Africa for almost twenty years. He brought his wife there to live with him. He became a leader for the Indians living there. He worked hard to make life easier for them. He started a newsletter and bought a farm where Indians worked together to help each other. They made their own clothes and farmed the land. They grew oranges and ground their own wheat to make bread.

The South African government made Indians pay a special tax. Gandhi told them not to pay it. The Indians listened to him. When Gandhi refused to pay the tax, a man named General Smuts put him in jail. Gandhi didn't mind being in jail. He used the time to think and to read books. He also made sandals, which he had learned to make on his farm. Finally, public outrage forced Smuts to let Gandhi go.

Gandhi didn't leave South Africa until the government passed a law granting freedom to the Indians.

As a sign of forgiveness, Gandhi sent General Smuts a pair of the sandals he had made in prison.

Gandhi found a new way to fight against evil. He called it *satyagraha,* which means "truth force." Many people call this "peaceful resistance." Gandhi did not believe in fighting with guns or even your hands. He believed that the best way to fight someone is—just don't do what they want you to do.

Back in India

When Gandhi returned to India in 1911, the British still ruled the country. The British had been interested in India for its wealth of spices, cloth, and other materials. They took these products from India and forced the people to buy them back at higher prices.

Gandhi wanted the British to give India back to his people. He wanted Indians to rule their own country. For the rest of his life he worked to reach this goal.

But, above all else, Gandhi wanted all the people in this new India to be equal. There would be no more Untouchables.

Gandhi made lots of money as a lawyer, but he decided to live very simply. This was hard on his wife and family. He gave away his money to help the poor. He walked every place he went. The only clothes he wore were sandals and a *dhoti*, which is like a pair of shorts. He traveled around the country to meet people and find out what they needed.

Gandhi was a small, thin man who wore eyeglasses. Everyone in India came to love him. They called him "Mahatma," which means "Great Soul." Many people thought he was a saint because he was so good.

Gandhi was not comfortable with people viewing him as a saint. He often joked about it. Once a man who rode on a train with Gandhi fell off the platform, but wasn't hurt. The man claimed he wasn't hurt because he had been sitting next to a saint. Gandhi said, "If that were true, you should not have fallen at all!"

Gandhi felt that for India to be free, his people must not buy any British goods. He told them not to buy clothes made in England. Everywhere he went he gave people spinning wheels so they could make their own clothes. He wanted his people to become self-sufficient so they would no longer need the British.

Everyone needs salt. Salt forms all along the coast of India. It comes from the ocean. The British would not allow the Indians to gather this salt. The British had companies that collected the salt and sold it back to the Indians.

Gandhi did not like this system. He led what came to be called the "Salt March." Thousands of people walked with him down to the sea. There, he picked up a handful of salt. All of his followers did the same. The British government arrested them. Even when Gandhi was arrested, the people did as he asked. They continued to resist the British, but they never fought back.

"What I did was a very simple thing. I declared that the British could not order me around in my own country." — *Gandhi*

Man of the Year

Gandhi was chosen by *Time* magazine to be "Man of the Year" in 1931. He was one of the most important people in the whole world. But he continued to live simply. He was still fighting for India's freedom, but the British would not let go of the country.

Once Gandhi went to England to meet the prime minister. He wore only his *dhoti* shorts, sandals, and a shawl. Someone asked him if he felt he had underdressed. Gandhi said, "No, the prime minister was wearing enough for both of us."

When World War II started, the British expected India to be on their side. But the Indians were tired of helping the British. Gandhi wanted the British out of India. He was afraid the Japanese might attack India to get back at the British.

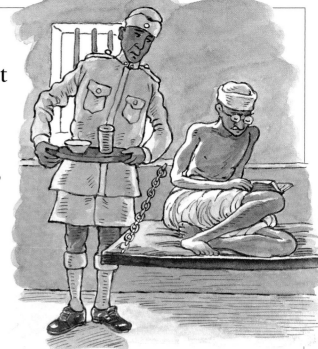

Gandhi was sent to prison again for stirring up trouble. While he was in prison, he refused to eat any food. Just as his mother had done, he *fasted*. After he hadn't eaten for many days, he became very weak. The British were afraid he might die, so they let him go.

After the war, in 1947, the British gave India its independence. All India celebrated. The president of the Indian congress called Gandhi the father of the Indian nation. Gandhi, with his walking staff, his round glasses, and his spinning wheel, had become the symbol of a free India.

But Gandhi stayed at home and read his books and prayed. He was pulling back from politics. He had always said he wanted to live to be 125, but now he wasn't so sure. Nearly 78 years old, he was tired from all his hard work.

Gandhi never gave up hope that India would win its independence: "I am always optimistic. I admit I do not see land in sight yet. But neither did Columbus, so it is said, until the last moment."

The Final Battle

Now that India was free, fighting broke out between two religious groups. The Muslims and the Hindus were fighting each other. The Muslims wanted a separate country of their own. Gandhi wanted everyone to live together in peace. But terrible battles broke out in the cities where both groups lived.

Gandhi went on another fast.

He told his people he would not eat until they stopped fighting. Three days later, Hindu, Muslim, and Christian leaders promised to get along. Gandhi took a drink of orange juice. His fast was over.

But in spite of Gandhi, the country did divide. The Hindus stayed in India. The Moslems formed a new country called Pakistan. This was a horrible time for all Indians. Millions of people were forced to give up their homes and businesses and move. Gandhi never recovered from this breaking up of India. He felt that he had not worked hard enough.

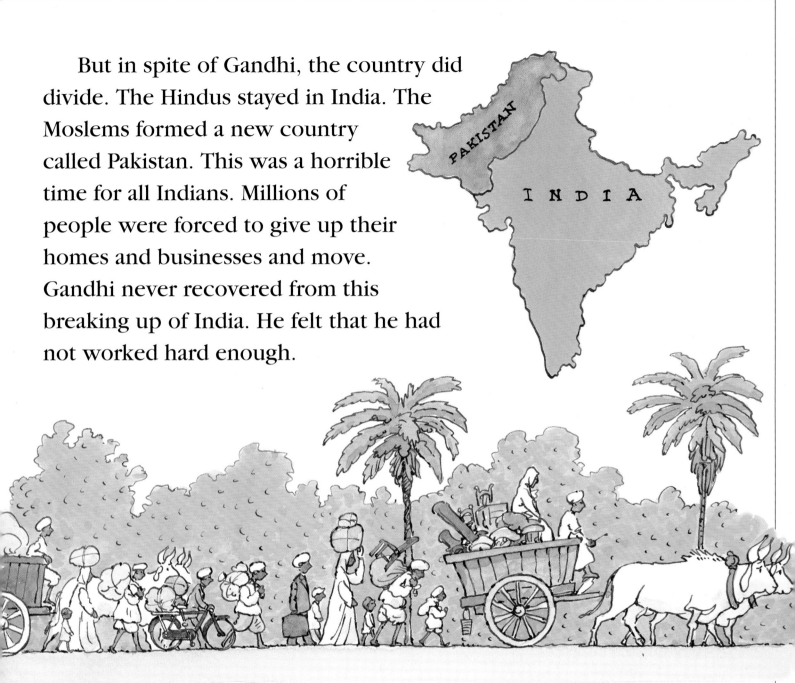

"The freedom of India means everything for us, but it also means much for the world. For freedom won through non-violence will mean the inauguration of a new order in the world." —*Gandhi*

Final Forgiveness

One day, Gandhi spoke to a follower. He said, "If someone tries to kill me, I will say God's name with my last breath. I will forgive them."

Three days later, on January 30, 1948, Gandhi went to lead a prayer meeting. A large number of his followers and friends were there to hear him. He walked among them to get to the platform. His hands were folded in a Hindu greeting. A Hindu man, someone

who blamed him for the division of India, came up to Gandhi. He aimed a pistol and shot him three times. As Gandhi died in the arms of his friends, he spoke God's name. With this word, he forgave his killer. The killer was captured and sentenced to death. Gandhi's sons did not want the man to die. They knew Gandhi would have been against that. Their father would have forgiven his murderer. No one listened to them. The man was hanged anyway.

"I cannot intentionally hurt anything that lives, much less human beings, even though they may do the greatest wrong to me." —*Gandhi*

His Funeral

Nearly half a million people walked in Gandhi's funeral march. His body was carried on a large military weapons carrier covered with flowers. Planes dropped flower petals down from the sky. All over the world, people mourned his death.

Gandhi is not forgotten, either in India or around the world. Most towns in India have a statue of Gandhi.

But much of what Gandhi fought for has not changed in India. There are still Untouchables—the poorest people, who cannot escape poverty. Women are still not treated well. Little girls are often left at orphanages because their families do not want them. The spinning wheel has been forgotten. India still buys most of its goods from rich, industrial countries.

But Gandhi gave the world a new way to handle violence. He lived a good and simple life. He asked hard questions and came up with some answers. He worked hard to help his people and free his country. He changed the world! Most importantly, he taught people to forgive each other.

"Generations to come, it may be, will scarce believe that such a one as this ever in flesh and blood walked upon this earth." —*Albert Einstein, speaking of Mahatma Gandhi*

Study Guide

Reading about famous or successful people can help us live our own lives. Sometimes we learn from their defeats, and sometimes we learn from their victories. Mahatma Gandhi's life was filled with both.

1. Which of these qualities do you think are most important?

Persistence   Kindness

Faith   Beauty

Strength   Curiosity

Courage   Trustworthiness

Imagination   Forgiveness

Honesty   Athletic ability

Patience   Intelligence

Humor   Gentleness

Which qualities do you think were most important to Gandhi?

2. The concept of forgiveness was very important to Gandhi. He always believed the best of everyone and gave them another chance. Have you ever forgiven someone? Has anyone ever forgiven you?

3. In the Hindu religion, society was divided into a caste system. Do we have a similar system in America? What groups is our society broken into?

4. Gandhi died in 1948, but many of his beliefs live on today. Some people think his way of *satyagraha*—peaceful resistance—would work only in India. Others think he was actually ahead of his time. We need to learn ways to get along with other countries to avoid going to war. Can you name an important American leader who was influenced by Gandhi?

5. Gandhi chose to live a simple life. He gave his money to the poor and wore only sandals and a *dhoti*. He lived in a small room and had very few possessions—a watch, a pair of glasses, and two eating bowls. Why do you think he chose to live this way?

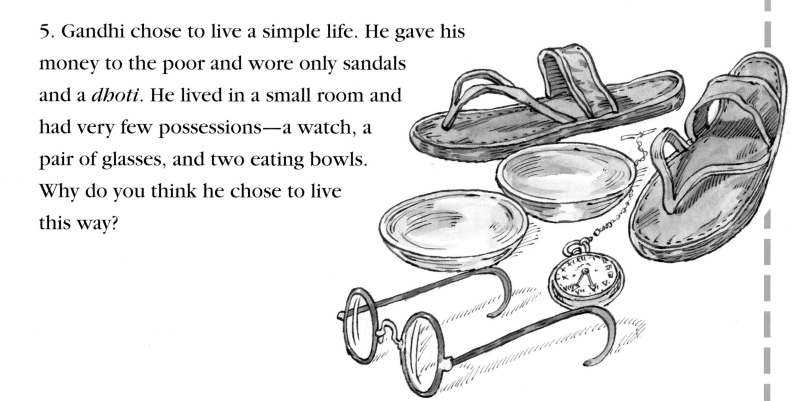

Study Guide Answers

1. Gandhi might have had a hard time answering this question. He needed many qualities to do what he did. Working for India's independence took great persistence and strength. Courage alone wasn't enough to help Gandhi get along peacefully with others. It took a lot of patience and forgiveness not to be angry with people who did not like him. Like Gandhi, we are all a mixture of many qualities.

2. We often forgive people without even thinking about it. If someone takes our seat on the bus and then apologizes to us, we say "that's all right." Sometimes, it's harder to forgive someone—like when they break something we love or call us a name. But if we do, it makes us feel better about ourselves.

3. American society is broken into economic levels—how much money people make. The "upper" class is made up people who have more than enough money. The "middle" class is made up of people who make enough money to be comfortable. The "lower" class includes people who either don't have jobs or don't make enough money to live comfortably. But people can move from one class to another.

4. Dr. Martin Luther King, Jr., was strongly influenced by Gandhi. At that time, blacks weren't allowed to eat in certain restaurants or ride at the front of the bus. Dr. King taught his people to fight discrimination in America the same way Gandhi had in India. Black Americans fought back by sitting at the front of the bus and by eating at any restaurant they wanted to.

5. When people want to own a lot of things—a new car, a fancy house, lots of jewelry—those possessions can actually own *them*. Gandhi wanted to be able to focus all his attention on helping the people of India. He didn't want anything to distract him. So he lived as simply as he could.

Mahatma Gandhi Time Line

1869 Mohandas Gandhi is born near Bombay, India.

1882 Young Gandhi and Kasturbai are married.

1887 Gandhi goes off to college in England. He studies law and becomes a lawyer.

1891 Gandhi returns home to India.

1893 Gandhi and his wife move to South Africa. He becomes a leader for the Indians living there.

1911 Gandhi returns to India. He decides to live simply and give his money away. He begins to fight for the rights of the Indian people.

1947 India wins its independence from the British.

January 30, 1948 Gandhi is killed at a prayer meeting.